A Glimmer in the Ordinary

Catherine Nash Weston

BookLeaf Publishing

India | USA | UK

Presentation by *BookLeaf Publishing*

Web: www.bookleafpub.com

E-mail: info@bookleafpub.com

ISBN: 9789358313765

First edition 2023

To my best friends, mum and dad, for always believing in me and cheering me on. And to my friend Camilla, for convincing me to take on this challenge and believing in me too, every step of the way.

PREFACE

A haiku is a traditional form of Japanese poetry consisting of three lines with a 5-7-5 syllable count. It often focuses on nature, seasons, or a fleeting moment, aiming to evoke a sense of simplicity and beauty. This format was chosen by the author as it aligns so well with the mission behind her collection of poems: to capture those small, everyday memories that live so vividly in her mind.

The Bookshop

Brief pause, light beckons,
Bookshop's glow, a soft delight,
Familiar invite.

Dawn Chorus

At the crack of dawn,
Feathered friends take early flight,
A singing choir.

The Stream

Sunlight on the stream,
Forest dances, water gleams,
Nature's whispers, dream.

Yellow

Sunshine, daffodils,
Lemons and lights, yellow is
hope and all things bright.

At the Seaside

Sea, sand, seagulls play,
The bright light of a sunny day,
Nature's dance on display.

Aeroplane

From up above the
World I see, an ocean of
Clouds aglow for me.

Purple

An ocean of lights
shines bright in the darkest of
nights, never alone.

Cats

Bright light, eyes constrict,
Cats' gaze, a twilight trick
Shadows dance, tails flick.

Rainbows

When the raindrops cease,
And the sun comes out to play,
Colours paint the sky.

Curiosity

A sighting of light,
Curiosity takes flight,
A life, imagined.

Stars

Stars in the night sky,
Each person, unique and bright,
Shine, you're special, fly.

Christmastime

Small electric lights,
For a moment all is right,
A Christmas delight.

Twilight

Twilight softly calls,
Daylight dims, a hush befalls,
Peace in stillness sprawls.

Bookworm

Cocooned in soft light,
Pages whisper tales at night,
Dreams take gentle flight.

Candles

Candlelight's soft glow,
Shadows dance on walls aglow,
Silent stories flow.

Lamplight

Under the lamplight,
Walking down a snowy street,
What a tranquil night.

Northern Lights

A soft hue from afar,
First a flicker, then a star,
Aurora's dance, bizarre.

Sleep

When night falls like ink,
Embraced by darkness, I sink,
Into dreams, I think.